Matthew Hale Carpenter

Before the Commission for Counting Presidential Votes

In the States where There are more than one Return from the Electoral

Colleges

Matthew Hale Carpenter

Before the Commission for Counting Presidential Votes
In the States where There are more than one Return from the Electoral Colleges

ISBN/EAN: 9783337404819

Printed in Europe, USA, Canada, Australia, Japan

Cover: Foto ©Suzi / pixelio.de

More available books at **www.hansebooks.com**

BEFORE THE

Commission for Counting Presidential Votes

IN THE

STATES WHERE THERE ARE MORE THAN ONE RETURN
FROM THE ELECTORAL COLLEGES,

1877.

*In the Matter of the Counting of the Votes given by the
Electoral College of Louisiana.*

MATT H. CARPENTER,

Of Counsel.

BEFORE THE

COMMISSION FOR COUNTING PRESIDENTIAL VOTES

IN THE

STATES WHERE THERE ARE MORE THAN ONE RETURN
FROM THE ELECTORAL COLLEGES,

˙1877.

In the Matter of the Counting of the Votes Given by the
Electoral College of Louisiana.

Constitution of the United Stattes.

The Constitution, article 2, section 1, provides that the
President shall be elected as follows:

" Each *State shall appoint, in such manner as the Legislature
thereof may direct*, a number of electors equal to the whole
number of Senators and Representatives to which the
State may be entitled in the Congress; but no Senator or
Representative, or person holding an office of trust or
profit under the United States, *shall be appointed* an
elector."

Amendments, article 12, provides as follows:

"The electors shall meet in their respective States, and
vote by ballot for President and Vice-President, one of
whom, at least, shall not be an inhabitant of the same
State with themselves; they shall name in their ballots the
person voted for as President, and in distinct ballots the
person voted for as Vice-President; and they shall make
distinct lists of all persons voted for as President, and of

all persons voted for as Vice-President, and of the number
of votes for each, which lists they shall sign and *certify*,
and transmit sealed to the seat of the Government of the
United States, directed to the President of the Senate;
the President of the Senate shall, in the presence of the
Senate and House of Representatives, open all *the certificates*,
and *the votes shall then be counted.* The person having the
greatest number of votes for President *shall be the President*, if such number be a majority of the whole number of
electors appointed."

ACTS OF CONGRESS.

Congress has provided (Rev. Stats., p. 21, sec. 131)
that "the electors of President and Vice-President shall be
appointed in each State on the Tuesday next after the first
Monday in November, in every fourth year," &c.

SEC. 133. "Each State may by law provide for the filling of any vacancies which may occur in its college of
electors, when such college meets to give its electoral
vote."

SEC. 134. "Whenever any State has held an election for
the purpose of choosing electors, and has failed to make a
choice on the day prescribed by law, the electors may be
appointed on a subsequent day in such manner as the legislature of such State may direct."

SEC. 135. "The electors for each State shall meet and
give their votes upon the first Wednesday in December in
the year in which they are appointed, at such place in such
State as the Legislature of such State shall direct."

.SEC. 136. "It shall be the duty of the executive of each
State to cause three lists of the names of the electors of such
State to be made and certified, and to be delivered to the
electors on or before the day on which they are required,
by the preceding section, to meet."

SEC. 142. "Congress shall be in session on the second
Wednesday in February succeeding every meeting of the
electors, and the certificates, or so many of them as have
been received, shall then be opened, the votes counted, and
the persons to fill the offices of President and Vice President ascertained and declared, agreeably to the Constitution."

The Legislature of the State of Louisiana, Oct. 19, 1868, (Laws 1868, p. 218), passed a general election law for the election of Governor, Lieutenant governor, members of the Legislature and other State and parish officers.

Sec. 32 of that act is as follows (page 223.)

Sec. 32. " *Be it further enacted, etc.*, That in every year in which an election shall be held for electors of President and Vice President of the United States, such election shall be held on the Tuesday next after the first Monday in the month of November, in accordance with an act of the Congress of the United States, approved January twenty-three, one thousand eight hundred and forty-five, entitled "An act to establish a uniform time for holding elections for electors of President and Vice President in all States of the Union." And such elections shall be held and conducted in the manner and form provided by law for general State elections."

Sec. 33. " *Be it further enacted, etc.*, That the foregoing provisions, except as to time and place of holding elections, shall apply to the election of all officers whose election is not otherwise provided for."

Eleven days afterwards, Oct. 30, 1868, the Legislature proceeded to, and "otherwise provided for" the election of Presidential electors, thus taking that election out of the operation of the General Election Law. The latter act is a complete regulation of Presidential electors, and is as follows :

No. 193.—An Act Relative to Presidential Electors.

" Section 1. *Be it enacted by the Senate and House of Representatives of the State of Louisiana in General Assembly convened,* That in every year in which an election is to be held for electors of President and Vice President of the United States, such election shall be held on Tuesday next after the first Monday in the month of November in such year in accordance with an act of the Congress of the United States approved January twenty-three, eighteen hundred and forty-five, entitled, ' An act to establish a uniform time for holding elections for electors of President

and Vice President in all of the States of the Union,' and
such elections shall be held and conducted in the manner
and form provided by law for general State elections."

" Sec. 2. *Be it further enacted, etc.*, *That every qualified
voter* in the State shall vote for seven persons as follows : "
"Two persons shall be selected from the State at large,
and one person shall be chosen from each congressional
district in this State ; and in case any ticket shall contain
two or more names of persons residing in the same district
(except the two chosen from the State at large) the first of
such names only shall be considered as duly voted for."

" Sec. 3, *Be it further enacted, etc.*, That no person shall
be an elector who is not a qualified voter in the district for
which he is chosen, or in case of being elected for the State
at large, then of some parish of the State.

" Sec. 4. *Be it further enacted, etc.*, That immediately after
the receipt of a return from each parish, or on the fourth
Monday of November, if the returns shall not sooner arrive,
the Governor, in presence of the Secretary of State, the Attorney General, a district judge of the district in which
the seat of government may be established, or any two of
them, shall examine the returns and ascertain therefrom
the several persons who have been duly elected electors.

"Sec. 5. *Be it further enacted, etc.*, That one of the returns from each parish, indorsed by the Governor, shall be
placed on file and preserved among the archives of the
Secretary of State,

" Sec. 6. *Be it further enacted, etc.*, That the names of the
persons selected, together with a copy of the returns from
the several parishes, shall forthwith be published in the
newspaper or papers in which the laws of the State may be
directed to be published.

" Sec. 7. *Be it further enacted, etc.*, That the electors shall
meet at the seat of government on the day appointed for
their meeting by the act of Congress, (the first Wednesday
in December,) and shall then and there proceed to execute
the duties and services enjoined upon them by the Constitution of the United States, in the manner therein prescribed.

" Sec. 8. *Be it further enacted, etc.*, That if any one or
more of the electors chosen by the people shall fail from
any cause whatever, to appear at the appointed place at the

hour of four p. m. of the day prescribed for their meeting, it shall be the duty of the other electors immediately to proceed by ballot to supply such vacancy or vacancies.

" Sec. 9. *Be it further enacted, etc.*, That each elector shall receive the same daily compensation and allowance which at that time shall be allowed by law to the members of the General Assembly, to be paid by the Treasurer of the State on warrants signed by the Governor.

" Sec. 10. *Be it further enacted, etc.*, That all laws conflicting herewith be, and the same are hereby, repealed; that this act shall take effect from and after its passage."

The Act of 1870.

March 16, 1870, the Legislature passed another election law. Laws of 1870, p, 145-161.

Section 35, page 150 of this act, reads as follows:

" Sec. 35. *Be it further enacted, etc.*, That in every year in which an election shall be held for the electors of President and Vice-President of the United States, such election shall be held on the Tuesday next after the first Monday in the month of November, in accordance with the act of the Congress of the United States approved January twenty-third, one thousand eight hundred and forty-five entitled 'An act to establish a uniform time for holding election for electors of President and Vice-President in all States of the Union,' and such election shall be held and conducted and returns made thereof in the manner and form prescribed by law for the general elections."

Section 38 of this act is as follows:

"Sec. 38. *Be it further enacted, etc.*, That the provisions of this act, except as to the time of holding elections, shall apply in the election of all officers whose election is not otherwise provided for."

The last section of said act is as follows:

"Sec. 85. *Be it further enacted, etc.*, That all laws or parts of law contrary to the provisions of this act and all laws *relating to the same subject-matter* are hereby repealed, and this act shall take effect from and after the passage."

REVISED STATUTES, 1870.

This revision took effect April 1, 1870. It contains a general-election law, differing materially from the act of 1870, and made no provisions for a returning board, and this revision also re-enacted the special act of 1868.

Section 1410 of the revision is as follows:

"SEC. 1410. In every year in which an election shall be held for electors of President and Vice-President of the United States, such election shall be held on the Tuesday next after the first Monday in the month of November, in accordance with an act of Congress of the United States approved Jan. 13th, 1845, entitled 'An act to establish a uniform time for holding elections for electors of President and Vice-President in all States of the Union,' and such elections shall be held and conducted in the manner and form provided by law for general State elections."

Sections 2823-2832 of the revision are the same in substance as the act of 1868. Section 2826 of the revision in relation to the canvass of votes given for presidential electors is as follows:

"SEC. 2826. Immediately after the receipt of a return from each parish, or on the fourth Monday of November if the returns should not sooner arrive, the Governor, in presence of the Secretary of State, the Attorney General, a district judge of the district in which the seat of government may be established, or any two of them, shall examine the returns, and ascertain therefrom the persons who have been duly elected electors."

Section 3990 of the revision repealed all former laws or parts of laws on the same subject-matter covered by the revision, with certain exceptions not material here.

THE ACT OF 1872.

Nov. 20, 1872, the Legislature passed another general election law, which was in force at the last November election. Sections 1, 29, 32, and 71 are as follows:

"SEC. 1. *Be it further enacted,* That all elections for State, parish, and judicial officers, members of the General

Assembly, and for members of Congress, shall he held on the first (Tuesday after the first) Monday in November; and said election shall be styled the general elections. They shall be held in the manner and form and subject to the regulations hereafter prescribed, and no other.

"Note.—By constitutional amendment, 1874, the day for holding general elections was changed from the first Monday to the first Tuesday following the first Monday in November.

"Sec. 29. *Be it further enacted, etc.*, That in every year in which an election shall be held for electors of President and Vice-President of the United States, such election shall be held at the time fixed by act of Congress.

"Sec. 32. *Be it further enacted, etc.*, That the provisions of this act, except as to the time of holding elections, shall apply in the election of all officers whose election is not otherwise provided for.

"Sec. 71. *Be it further enacted, etc.*, That this act shall take effect from and after its passage, and that all others on the subject of election laws be and the same are hereby repealed."

I.

The first questions naturally suggested by this discussion are, what is the character of this Tribunal, and what is the *nature* of the powers conferred upon it?

The Constitution of the United States embodies the American conception of a Republic. It creates a Government to exercise the powers of sovereignty over certain enumerated subjects. It proceeds upon the fundamental idea that the rights, privileges, and liberties of the people can only be secured against encroachment on the part of those charged with the execution of governmental powers by a careful separation of legislative, executive, and judicial powers, and a distribution of such powers among three great, equal, and co-ordinate departments. The legislative power is vested in the Congress, the executive power is vested in the President, and the judicial power is vested in one Supreme Court, and in such inferior courts as the

Congress may from time to time ordain and establish. "The judges, both of the Supreme and inferior courts, shall hold their offices during good behavior, and shall, at stated times, receive for their services, a stated compensation, which shall not be diminished during their continuance in office."

It is well settled that "the judicial power" cannot be vested elsewhere than in courts composed of judges holding their offices during good behavior.

It is therefore certain that no part of "the judicial power" can be vested in a Tribunal organized as this Tribunal is. No Tribunal created by act of Congress, whose decisions are subject to review except by other judicial courts of superior jurisdiction, can be considered as judicial courts. The Court of Claims, as originally constituted, could render judgments, so called; but such judgments were submitted to the approval and ultimate action of Congress. For this reason, the Supreme Court of the United States held that no appeal would lie from its decisions to the Supreme Court of the United States.

Gordon v. *The United States*, 2 Wall., 561.

After this decision, Congress remodeled that court, and gave conclusive effect to its judgment; since which appeals have been entertained by the Supreme Court of the United States.

In *The United States* v. *Ferriera*, 13 How., 40, an act of Congress had conferred upon the district judge of the United States for Florida authority to adjudicate upon certain claims arising under the treaty with Spain; which claims, when adjudicated by him, should be paid, *if the Secretary of the Treasury* should, on a report of the evidence, deem it equitable. The court, by Taney, C. J., say:

"The powers conferred by these acts of Congress upon the judge as well as the Secretary are, it is true, *judicial in their nature*, for judgment and discretion must be exercised by both of them. But it is nothing more than the power ordinarily given by law to a commissioner appointed to adjust claims to lands or money under a treaty, or special powers to inquire into or decide any other particular class of controversies in which the public or individuals may be concerned. A power of that description may constitutionally be conferred on a Secretary as well as on a commissioner. *But is not judicial* in either case *in the sense* in which judicial power is granted by the Constitution to the courts of the United States."

See also *Hayburn's Case*, 2 Dall., 409.

It is, therefore, plain from the provisions of the Constitution that the judicial power could not be vested in this Tribunal, and it is equally clear that the bill organizing this Tribunal does not pretend to clothe it with such power, because the decision, so called, which this Tribunal may render is submitted to the approval of and may be reversed by the two Houses of Congress.

What, then, is this Tribunal? It is, we submit, a mere legislative commission, exercising political power pertaining to the jurisdiction of Congress. Congress finds itself charged with the duty of ascertaining who, if any one, has been elected President of the United States, by the votes cast in ths several Electoral Colleges on the 6th of December last. And to aid it in the performance of this duty—the exercise of this political power—it has raised this commission to investigate, and decide, and report to the two Houses of Congress upon certain matters included in the performance of that duty; and the bill raising this commission provides that its report shall be made to the two Houses, and shall be conclusive, unless reversed by the Houses themselves.

There is no doubt of the power of both Houses of Congress by law, or perhaps by a joint resolution, to create a commission to investigate and report upon any subject falling within the scope of ordinary legislation, or relating to the performance of any duty cast upon Congress by the Constitution. Similar parliamentary commissions frequently occur in English history; sometimes raised by

2

the Houses themselves from their own members, and sometimes authorized by statute and appointed by the Crown. For instance, by statute, 15 and 16 Vict., ch. 57, a commission was authorized, which was appointed by the Crown to enquire into alleged corrupt practices in elections of members of the House of Commons, which commission was authorized by the statute to send for persons and papers, administer oaths, examine witnesses, etc. And false swearing before such commission would have been perjury under the laws of Great Britain. This commission made report, which was made the foundation for legislation upon that important subject.

May's Par. Prac., p. 593.

The Constitution, amendment XII, provides, in regard to the votes given in the several Electoral Colleges, that they shall be certified and returned to the President of the Senate, and then provides as follows:

" The President of the Senate shall, in the presence of the Senate and House of Representatives, open all the *certificates*, AND THE VOTES SHALL THEN BE COUNTED."

But by whom the votes shall be counted, the Constitution does not declare. Most of the powers conferred by the Constitution of the United States are conferred upon some designated department or officer. There are other powers, however, conferred upon the United States generally. For instance, article 4, section 4, provides as follows:

"The United States shall guarantee to every State in this Union a republican form of government, and shall protect each of them against invasion, and on application of the Legislature or of the Executive, (when the Legislature cannot be convened,) against domestic violence."

The last clause of the Legislative article confers upon Congress the power—

" To make all laws which shall be necessary and proper for carrying into Execution the foregoing Powers, and all other powers rested by this Constitution in the Government of the United States, or in any Department or Office thereof."

Congress has provided by law for the execution of the power as to protection against domectic violence by the President.

The constitutionality of the bill creating this commission may be considered upon one or the other of two grounds.

(1) If the power to count the votes is vested in the two houses of Congress, then this commission is a proper instrumentality for making the necessary investigation to enable the two houses intelligently to execute the power. If on the other hand the case is to be treated as one of power granted generally—that is, without designation as to who shall perform it—then it falls within the power of Congress to make laws for its execution as a power vested by the Constitution in the Government of the United States, or in some department or officer thereof. If the latter is the true view of the Constitution, then Congress might pass a law creating a commission or court, to be appointed by the President to count the votes, and leave the matter entirely to them.

But, evidently, the bill proceeds upon the theory that the votes are to be counted by the two houses of Congress, because by the bill power is reserved to the two houses to set aside the report—called the decision—to be made by this commission. And considering the matter in this light it is manifest that Congress may impose upon the commission such duties—that is, order it to investigate such questions as it may see fit. It may direct the commission to report what is the *prima facie* right of either candidate appearing from the face of certain papers, or it may direct this commission to ascertain and report upon the real *de jure* right of the several candidates.

What duty, then, does the law creating this tribunal impose upon it? The law declares that you shall—

"By a majority of votes decide whether any and what

votes from such State are the votes provided for by the Constitution of the United States, *and how many and what persons were duly appointed electors in such State?*"

Inasmuch as by the Constitution no person can cast a vote for President who has not been duly appointed an elector, it would undoubtedly have been sufficient to provide that this tribunal should decide "what votes from such State are the votes provided for by the Constitution." But for greater certainty, and to end all question, it is further expressly provided that this tribunal shall decide "how many and what persons were duly appointed electors in such State."

And to enable you to perform this duty, the act clothes you with all the powers of the two Houses of Congress. What this means may be inferred from the fact that the two Houses of Congress in the last count of presidential votes concurred in deciding that the electoral vote of the Louisiana college ought to be excluded, because the votes cast at the popular election for electors had not been canvassed according to the laws of that State; thus going behind a regular certificate of the Governor that the electors had been duly appointed, and a regular return of the votes cast by said college. This is at least a construction by the two Houses themselves of their power to go behind the certificate of the Governor to ascertain whether, the electors had been duly appointed. It will be said that this was under the 22d joint rule of the two Houses. It seems to be a matter of dispute between the two Houses to-day whether or not that rule is now in force; but whether it is or not, is wholly immaterial. Either House, or the two Houses, may regulate practice in the exercise of their constitutional authority; but neither, nor both, can add to that authority by rules of their own. If this joint rule added to the Constitution, it was void; if it took from the Constitution, it was void; if it did neither, it was useless. And the concurrent action of both Houses of Congress, in rejecting the vote of Louisiana four years ago, must be regarded as a declaration by them of their power in the premises, and that power they have confered upon this tribunal.

This tribunal has been created to meet a great national emergency. The public welfare and business interests alike require a speedy, final, and satisfactory settlement of the presidential question. The people will be content with, and the rival candidates will acquiesce in, any determination of the question founded upon the full merits of the case. But no one will be content with, no candidate will acquiesce in, a determination of this great question which ignores the merits and rests upon technicalities or false certificates.

It is a total error to suppose that this tribunal can make any decision which, in the judicial sense of that term, can settle this question. And it is an equal error to suppose that Congress has pretended to clothe this tribunal with any such power.

On the contrary, section 6 of this bill reserves to the defeated candidate the right—if any such right now exists by law—to prosecute a writ of *quo warranto* against the candidate who may be counted in. It has been settled in England for more than one hundred years, and is perfectly well settled in this country, that information in the nature of *quo warranto* is in its *nature* a civil proceeding, and must be so classified in the distribution of cases between courts of civil and courts of criminal jurisdiction.

Rex v. *Francis*, 2 *D. & E.*, 484.

In *State Bank* v. *The State*, 1 *Blackford*, 272, the court said : " We have no need of resorting to the general doctrine or information, for a *quo warranto* on information is a criminal proceeding only in name and in form ; in its *nature* it is *purely a civil proceeding.*"

Citing 2 *Kid on Corpo.*, 439.

King v. *Francis*, 2 *T. R.*, 484.

" The proceeding by information in the nature of a *quo war-*

ranto is essentially a civil proceeding, and the pleadings in it are as much subject to amendment as they are in ordinary civil actions. It is criminal only in form."

State of Florida v. *Gleason, Flor.*, 109.

In *Brison* v. *Lingo*, 26 *Mo.*, 496, the Supreme Court said : "The inquiry arises, is this a criminal case? For a great while it has been applied to the simple purpose of trying civil right, and regarded as a remedy to try the right to office." The court held it was a civil case.

See also *State* v. *Kupfurle*, 44 *Mo.*, 154.

A proceeding by *quo warranto* is not a criminal proceeding. *Ensminger* v. *Peo*, 47 *Ill.*, 384.

In *Commonwealth* v. *Browne*, 1 *S. & R.*, 382, it was held that "an information in the nature of a *quo warranto*, although a *criminal* proceeding in *form*, is in *substance* but a *civil* one; and is therefore not within the prohibition of the 10th article of the Constitution of Pennsylvania."

In *State ex rel.*, *Bashford* v. *Barstow*, 4 *Wis.*, 567, the Attorney General, after some proceedings, filed a formal discontinuance on the part of the State, but the court held the suit must proceed as between the relator and the defendant, and the court proceeded and rendered judgment in favor of the relator ; and he thereupon entered into and held the office for the balance of the term.

The Constitution of the United States, art. 3, sec. 2, declares that the judicial power of the United States "shall extend to all cases arising under this Constitution, the laws of the United States, and treaties made under their authority," etc.

A contest between Mr. Tilden, if he shall be counted out, and Mr. Hayes, if he shall be counted in, touching the right to exercise the office of President, would undoubtedly be a case arising under the Constitution and laws of the United States.

The act of Congress March 3, 1875, 18 Statutes at Large, Part 3, provides as follows :

"That the Circuit Courts of the United States shall have original cognizance, concurrent with the courts of the several States, of all suits of a *civil nature* at common law or in equity, where the matter in dispute exceeds, exclusive of costs, the sum or value of five hundred dollars, and arising under the Constitution or laws of the United States, or treaties made, or which shall be made, under their authority," &c.

It is well settled that where the title to an office is in dispute the amount involved, for the purpose of jurisdiction, is the salary of the office.

U. S. v. *Addison*, 22 *How.*, 174.

It is true the act of Congress quoted above says nothing about writ or information, of *quo warranto*. But when an act of Congress confers upon a Circuit Court jurisdiction of a case or controversy, the power of the court to issue the proper writ, or entertain the proper proceedings to bring the case or controversy before the court, cannot be questioned.

It is well settled that in proceedings by *quo warranto* the court will ascertain the right to the office and go through all forms, fictions, certificates of canvassing boards and commissions of office to ascertain that right.

People v. *Van Slyck*, 4 *Cow.*, 297.
People v. *Ferguson*, 8 *Cow.*, 102.
Jeter v. *State*, 1 *McCord*, 233.
People v. *Vail*, 20 *Wend.*, 12.
Bashford v. *Barstow*, 4 *Wis.*, 567.
Hill v. *State*, 1 *Ala.*, (*N. S.*,) 559.

As a determination of this question by this tribunal based upon the broad merits of the case would give peace to the country and set the obstructed wheels of enterprise once more in motion, so, on the other hand, a narrow and technical decision which would throw the question into a judicial controversy to continue for months would be a calamity to the country and cast a shadow upon the efficiency of free institutions.

This is undoubtedly the reason why Congress has directed this commission to inquire into the ultimate, final fact as a court of law would do on a *quo warranto*—reserving to itself, however, the right to adopt or reject such conclusion in the final counting of votes, which is to be done by the two Houses themselves after this commission shall have performed its functions. The duty cast upon this commission to inquire and decide—that is, report—what persons were "*duly* appointed electors" can be satisfied in no way but by an inquiry into the ultimate fact; that is, the legality of such appointment. This commission must take judicial notice of the laws of Louisiana. (*Penington* v. *Gibson*, 16 *How.*, 65.) It must therefore ascertain whether any law of that State directs the manner in which electors shall be appointed; whether such State law is in accordance with the Constitution of that State, and whether in fact the electors were appointed according to such law. Without this it is impossible to say whether or not they were *duly* appointed.

II.

Whether the election law of 1870 was repealed by the revision, or whether it remained in force after April 1, 1870, when the revision took effect, depends upon the effect to be given to several acts of the legislature enacted at the session of 1870.

On the 28th February, 1870, the following act was passed:

"No. 50. An act giving precedence in authority to all the other acts and joint resolutions passed by the general assembly at this session over the acts known as 'The Revision of the Statutes and of the Civil Code and Code of Practice' when there exists any conflict in the provisions of said acts and revisions.

"SECTION 1. *Be it enacted by the Senate and House of Representatives of the State of Louisiana in general assembly convened*, That all the acts and joint resolutions passed during the *present session* of the general assembly which may be contrary to or in any manner conflict with the acts of the present session known as '*Revision of the Statutes* of a general character, and of the Civil Code and Code of Practice,' shall have precedence of said revisions, and be held as the law in opposition thereto, and as repealing those acts so far as they may be in opposition or conflict."—*Promulgated March* 20, 1870.

On the 14th March, 1870, the revision was passed, and by its terms was to go into effect April 1, 1870.

On the 16th March, 1870, the election law was passed, to take effect from its passage.

The question is whether after the 1st April the revision repealed the election law of 1870, or whether the election law of 1870, by virtue of the act of February 28, 1870, remained in force notwithstanding the revision, and nullified the general election law contained in the revision. The general rule is that an act passed to take effect on a future day, has on that day the same effect as though it had been *passed on that day*.

"A law speaks from the time of its going into effect."

> *Rice* v. *Ruddiman*, 10 *Mich.*, 125.
> *Peo.* v. *Johnson*, 6 *Cal.*, 673.
> *Arthur* v. *Franklin*, 16 *Ohio N. S.*, 193.
> *Lyner* v. *Stale*, 8 *Ind.*, 490.
> *Supervisors* v. *Keady*, 34 *Ill.*, 293.
> *Charless* v. *Lamberson*, 1 *Clarke*, (*Iowa*,) 435.
> *Price* v. *Hopkins*, 13 *Mich.*, 318.

Treating the revision as having been passed April 1, 1870, the time when by its own terms it was to take effect, it repealed the election law of 1870, and also repealed all prior acts denying to it the full force and effect which would otherwise attach to it as a law. And this I believe to be the sound view of the subject.

But if it is competent for the Legislature to provide that

3

of two acts thereafter to be passed the first shall repeal the second, then the revision taking effect April 1st, 1870, was subordinated to the election law of March 16, 1870.

It is not very material to this case which view of this matter shall be taken by the court. It is certain that the act of 1868, re-enacted in the revision, *was* or it *was not* in force at the last election.

I shall present the case first upon the ground that the act of 1868 was in force, as I incline to that opinion.

(1.) Assuming the act of 1868 (re-enacted in the revision of 1870) as in force, it is not pretended that the votes given for electors at the last election in that State have ever been canvassed as required by this act. It is evident that the canvass which was made, and which resulted in the exclusion of over 6,000 votes in favor of the Tilden electors, was not only unauthorized by this act, but in direct violation of its express provisions.

By this law, section 2826, it is provided that—

"*Immediately* after the receipt of a return from *each parish*, or on the fourth Monday of November if the returns should not sooner arrive, the *Governor* in the presence of the Secretary of State, the Attorney General, a district judge of the district in which the seat of government may be established, or any two of them, shall examine *the returns*, and ascertain *therefrom* the persons who have been duly elected electors.

"Sec. 2827. One of the returns *from each parish*, indorsed by the Governor, shall be placed on file and preserved among the archives of the Secretary of State.

"Sec. 2828. The names of persons elected, together with a copy of the returns *from the several parishes*, shall forthwith be published in the newspaper or papers in which the laws of the State may be directed to be published."

Under this law no returns whatever could be excluded. The result must be ascertained from all the returns "from each parish." No judicial power and no discretion is conferred by this act; the duty is purely mathematical. The returns from each parish are to be preserved among the archives of the Secretary of State. It will not be pretended by any one that if this law was in force the election was conducted and returned according to its provisions. If the election law of 1868, as re-enacted in the revision of April 1, 1870, was not repealed by the act of March 16, 1870, then it certainly was in force at the time of the election, unless repealed by the act of 1872. The history of this act of 1872 is well known. In the early part of 1872 the Legislature passed this bill and sent it to Governor Warmoth for his approval. He neither approved or vetoed the bill during the session of the Legislature. But after the presidential and the State elections of November, 1872, when Governor Warmouth was engaged in a contest with Judge Durrell, months after the adjournment of the Legislature which passed the bill, and after Judge Durrell in the Circuit Court of the United States had tied up the canvass of those elections, Governor Warmoth, as the only means of counteracting the usurpations of a Federal judge, took this act of 1872 from his pocket and pretended to give it his approval, and caused it to be promulgated as a law of the State.

The repealing clause contained in this act is very sweeping in terms, but was evidently intended to repeal only the general election laws of the State. An examination of these statutes will show that the Legislature always treated the election of electors as a matter distinct from the general elections of the State.

In 1868 the Legislature, on the 19th of October, passed an act entitled "An act relative to elections in the State of Louisiana," &c., and on the 30th day of the same month passed another act entitled an act—

"Relative to presidential electors," and both were published in the session laws of that year as distinct and independent acts.

In the Revised Statutes of 1870 the general election law of the State is published under the head "Elections," on pages 272–282; under the head of "Presidential Electors," on pages 550–553, is published the act of 1868,

Here the intention is manifest to treat the two elections as distinct, and they are regulated by different provisions. The election of State officers under the authority of the State constitution, and the election of electors under the authority of the Constitution and laws of the United States, are treated in the laws of Louisiana as distinct subjects, and, notwithstanding the repealing clause of the act of 1872 is very broad, it is evident from the whole act that it was only intended to repeal all laws relating to general elections under State authority. It is a well-established rule for the interpretation of statutes, that, for the purpose of ascertaining the intention of the Legislature in any particular part of the act, the whole act must be considered; and if the general intention manifested by the whole act is clear, such intention will enable the court to control the *language* of other parts of the act.

Blanchard v. *Sprague*, 3 *Sumner*, 279.

"In doubtful cases a court should compare all the *parts* of a statute, *and different statutes in pari materia*, to ascertain the intention of the Legislature."

The Elizabeth, 1 *Paine*, 10.

"Words which, standing alone in an act of Congress, may properly be understood to pass a beneficial interest in land, will not be regarded as having that effect *if the context shows that they were not intended to be so used*."

Rice v. *Railroad Co.*, 1 *Black*, 358.

That the act of 1872 was intended as a regulation *only* of the election, for *State* officers, and the repeal of former laws upon that subject, is manifest from the first section of that act.

"SECTION 1. That all elections for *State, parish*, and *judicial* officers, members of the General Assembly, and for members of Congress, shall be held on the first Monday in November, and said election shall be styled the *general elections*. They shall be held in the manner and form and subject to the regulations hereinafter prescribed, *and in no other*."

Presidential electors are not State officers. As between
the Union and the States to determine whether an officer
is a Federal or State *officer*, we have only to determine
whether the *office* is created by the Constitution and laws
of the Union or the constitution and laws of a State. Senators are elected by the Legislatures of the States, but the
office is created by the Constitution of the United
States, and nobody doubts that a Senator is an officer
of the United States and not of the State which elects
him. The office of elector is created by the Constitution
of the United States. The office is therefore a Federal
office and the fact that a State may fill the office by
appointment does not change the character of the office.
Suppose an amendment of the Constitution to be adopted
to-morrow, providing that in addition to the present number each State might appoint an additional judge of the
Supreme Court of the United States, would it be pretended
that a judge thus appointed was any less an officer of the
United States than the other judges appointed by the
President? The effect of the Constitution is simply this:
it establishes an office and authorizes a State to fill it. The
only power possessed by the State in regard to the electoral
college for each State is the power of appointment; but
in what manner the *duties of the office* shall be performed,
when the electors shall meet, and how they shall vote, the
manner and order of their proceedings, the authentication
of their action, and how to make return to the General
Government, whether they shall give bonds or take oaths
and receive compensation, and indeed all things concern-
ing the office except the filling of the office are subjects of
Federal regulation; subjects over which the State has no
control whatever.

Again, the act of 1872 contains no direction in regard to
the manner of appointing electors. It does not declare,
nor does any other law of the State, except that of 1868,
whether the electors shall be chosen by the people, elected
by the Legislature, or appointed by the Governor. The act

of 1868 is a specific and complete regulation of the whole subject, and provides for the election of electors by a popular vote; and provides that, in case of the absence of any of the electors, the other electors may supply their place by ballot; that two electors shall be elected at large, and one from each Congressional district; and provides how the votes given shall be canvassed and certified. The act of 1872 contains *no* provision upon any of these subjects, and only refers to electors for the purpose of fixing the time for the appointment, a provision wholly useless, because Congress, and not the State, must fix the time for making such appointment. All that the State can do is to direct, by its Legislature, the manner in which, and not the time at which, the appointment shall be made, when the time arrives for making it as provided by Congress.

It is not to be supposed that the Legislature, in the act of 1872, intended to strike down the only act regulating the manner for appointing Presidential electors, without making any other provision covering the subject.

Again, the act of Congress (Rev. Stats., p. 21, sec. 133) provides as follows:

" SEC. 133. Each State may, *by law*, provide for the filling of any vacancies which may occur in its college of electors when such college meets to give its electoral vote."

The act of 1868 provides that when the electoral college meets if any elector is absent his place may be filled by the electors present, they voting by ballot. But the act of 1872 provides, (sec. 24):

" That *all elections* to be held in this State to fill *any vacancies* shall be conducted and managed, and returns thereof shall be made, *in the same manner as is provided for general elections.*"

Now, if this act of 1872 be construed as repealing the act of 1868, in regard to the election and returns for election of electors, then, beyond question, a vacancy in the electoral college would be one of the vacancies provided for in the section last quoted; and *such vacancy* could only be filled by another popular election.

In the case at bar, when the Electoral College in Louisiana convened it was found that two of the electors had been holding offices of " honor or trust " under the United States at the time of the election, and therefore the election as to them was void under the provisions of the Constitution of the United States. We contend here that this was not a vacancy, but was a case falling within section 134 of the Revised Statutes of the United States; in other words, there had been a failure to make a choice as to them, and no law of the State, not even the law of 1868, provided for appointment to fill their places. But the Electoral College treated the case as one of vacancy, and proceeded by election to fill the places deemed vacant. Treating this as a case of vacancy, and not a case of a failure to elect, it was a regular proceeding under the act of 1868, but utterly void if that act was repealed by the act of 1872, because the language in the act of 1872, in regard to filling vacancies, is as broad as other parts of the act in regard to the election of officers. And it is impossible for this tribunal to hold that the act of 1872 repealed the act of 1868 in regard to the election of electors, but that the section last quoted did not repeal the section in the act of 1868, which authorized a different method of filling a vacancy in the particular case.

III.

But if the election law of March 16, 1870, survived the effect of the Revised Statutes, April 1, 1870, then the act of 1868 was repealed, and there was no law in force in that State at the last election directing the manner of appointing Presidential electors.

It is very clear that the election law of 1870 repealed the act of 1868.

The act of 1870, after providing a method of holding, conducting, and returning the general elections of the State, provided, in section 35, that the election for electors should be held on the day fixed by the act of Congress, and provided as follows: "and such elections shall be held and conducted, and returns made thereof, *in the manner and form prescribed by law for the general elections.*"

And the last section of the act provided as follows:

"That all laws or parts of laws contrary to the provisions of this act, *and all laws relating to the same subject-matter*, are hereby repealed, and that this act shall take effect from and after its passage."

The special act of 1868 was, by implication, in part *at least*, repealed by the 85*th section* of this act, which made different provision for holding, conducting, and returning the election. Even conceding that the portion of the act of 1868 which declared who should be voters and who should be voted for, might *have stood with* the 35th section of this act, and therefore not have been repealed by this section; yet it is *impossible* to hold that *any part* of the act of 1868 escaped the effect of the repealing clause of this act of 1870, because it is evident that the 85th section of the act of 1870 and the act of 1868 were "*laws relating to the same subject-matter.*"

IV.

It is immaterial, so far as practical results are concerned, whether this court hold the act of 1868 to have been in force or not at the last election, because in either case votes enough to change the result must be excluded from the votes given by the Hayes electors. If the act of 1868 was in force, then there has been no canvass according to law of the votes cast for electors, and all the votes given by the Hayes Electors must be rejected, as they were four years ago by both Houses of Congress, for the same reason. If the act of 1868 was not in force, then there was no law directing the manner of appointment of electors, and all the votes given by the Hayes electors must be rejected for that reason. Because it is evident that if a State has omitted through its Legislature to provide the manner in which electors shall be appointed, or, having made such provision, repeals it and makes no other, no constitutional appointment can be made by such State.

And if this were otherwise, still the two votes given by the two persons elected by the Electoral College to fill the supposed vacancies must be excluded.

V.

Although we are entirely confident that the vote of Louisiana must be excluded for the reasons before given, yet should the court differ with us in regard to the objections before made, and hold that the act of 1872 repealed the act of 1868 and is itself a complete regulation of the subject of appointment of electors, still we submit that the rejection of over 6,000 Tilden votes by the Returning Board under the provisions of the act of 1872 was wholly unauthorized by that act, and void. This brings us to consider the act of 1872 according to its own provisions in regard to the jurisdiction and powers of the Returning Board. Section 3 of this act is as follows:

"Sec. 3. *Be it further enacted, etc.*, That in such canvass and compilation the returning officers shall observe the following order: They shall compile first the statements from all polls or voting places at which there shall have been a fair, free, and peaceable registration and election. Whenever from any poll or voting place there shall be received the statement of any supervisor of registration or commissioner of election *in form* as required by *section twenty-six* of this act, on affidavit of three or more citizens, of any riot, tumult, acts of violence, intimidation, armed disturbance, bribery, or corrupt influences, which prevented or tended to prevent a fair, free, and peaceable vote of all qualified electors entitled to vote at such poll or voting place, such returning officers shall not canvass, count, or compile the statements of votes from such poll or voting place until the statements from all other polls or voting places shall have been canvassed and compiled. The returning officers shall then proceed to investigate the statements of riot, tumult, acts of violence, intimidation, armed disturbance, bribery, or corrupt influences at any such poll or voting place; and if from the evidence of

4

such statement they shall be convinced that such riot, tumult, acts of violence, intimidation, armed disturbance, bribery, or corrupt influences did not materially interfere with the purity and freedom of the election at such poll or voting place, or did not prevent a sufficient number of qualified voters thereat from registering or voting to materially change the results of the election, then, and not otherwise, said returning officers shall canvass and compile the vote of such poll or voting place with those previously canvassed and compiled; but if said returning officers shall not be fully satisfied thereof, it shall be their duty to examine further testimony in regard thereto, and to this end they shall have power to send for persons and papers. If, after such examination, the said returning officers shall be convinced that said riot, tumult, acts of violence, intimidation, armed disturbance, bribery, or corrupt influences did materially interfere with the purity and freedom of the election at such poll or voting place, or did prevent a sufficient number of the qualified electors thereat from registering and voting to materially change the result of the election, then the said returning officers shall not canvass or compile the statement of the votes of such poll or voting place, but shall exclude it from their returns: *Provided*, That any person interested in said election by reason of being a candidate for office shall be allowed a hearing before said returning officers upon making application within the time allowed for the forwarding of the returns of said election.''

Section 26 of this act is as follows:

"SEC. 26. *Be it further enacted, etc.*, That in any parish, precinct, ward, city or town, in which, during the time of registration or revision of registration, or on any day of election, there shall be any riot, tumult, acts of violence, intimidation and disturbance, bribery or corrupt influences at any place within said parish, or at or near any poll or voting place or place of registration, or revision of registration, which riot, tumult, acts of violence, intimidation and disturbance, bribery or corrupt influences shall prevent, or tend to prevent a fair, free, peaceable and full vote of all the qualified electors of said parish, precinct, ward, city or town, it shall be the duty of the commissioners of election, if such riot, tumult, acts of violence, intimidation and disturbance, bribery or corrupt influences occur on the day of election, or of the supervision of registration of the parish, if they occur during the time of registration or revision of registration, to make in duplicate and under oath a *clear and full statement of all the facts relating thereto*, and of the *effect* produced by such riot, tumult, acts of violence, intimidation and disturbance, bribery or corrupt influences in preventing a fair, free, peaceable, and full registration or election, *and of the number* of qualified electors deterred by such riots, tumult, acts of violence, intimidation and disturbance, bribery or corrupt influences from registering or voting, which statement shall also be corroborated under oath by three respectable citizens, qualified electors of the parish. When such statement is made by a commissioner of election or a supervisor of registration, he shall forward it in duplicate to the supervisor of registration of the parish, if in the city of New Orleans, to the Secretary of State, one copy of which, if made to the supervisor of registration, shall be forwarded by him to the returning officers provided for in section 2 of this act when he makes the returns of election in his parish. His copy of said statement shall be so annexed to his returns of elections by paste, wax, or some adhesive substance, that the same can be kept together, and the other copy the supervisor of registration shall deliver to the clerk of the court of his parish for the use of the district attorney.''

We contend that the action of the Returning Board in excluding from their canvass over 6,000 votes for the Tilden electors was void, *even if the provisions of this act repeal the act of* 1868, for the following reasons :

1. The Constitution of the United States provides that " each *State* shall appoint, in such manner as the Legislature thereof may direct, a number of electors, equal to the whole number," &c.

When the Constitution refers to a State it refers, of course, to a State of this Union—a community organized under a State constitution republican in form. When the Constitution of the United States was adopted the States were communities organized according to the American idea of republics. One of the most important and essential features of a Republican government, according to the American idea, is a separation of legislative, judicial, and executive functions, and a distribution of such powers among separate and distinct departments. One of the duties imposed upon the Federal Government is to guarantee to every State in this Union a republican form of government. And, of course, in admitting new States it is the duty of Congress to see that such is the form of their government. As it is the duty of the United States to guarantee—that is, see to it that every State has a republican form of government—it follows that the government of a State, its form, structure, and powers must constantly be in the Federal mind. And the provision of the Constitution that each State shall appoint electors must be construed to mean that such State, according to the provisions of its own constitution, shall appoint electors. No State could delegate this power to another State or to a foreign prince or power, or to individuals, by name or classifying designation. It is only *the State*—the constitutional republican State—a State of this Union in its written republican form of government, proceeding acording to of its constitution, which constitution is constantly subject to Federal supervision, that can appoint an elector. In other words, when the Constitution provides that each State shall appoint electors, it means, of course, that it shall appoint them according to its own constitution and laws. And what its *laws* may be must be determined by its own constitution, which, on the admission of the State, has been approved by Congress; and which, in all its mutations by amendments, continues to enjoy the approval of Congress as a republican form of government. And when the Constitution of the United States declares that " each State shall appoint, in such manner as the Legislature thereof may direct, a number of electors," &c., it does in substance provide that the State shall prescribe a manner for such appointment in accordance with its own constitution. The Federal Government knows that any act of a State legislature in violation of its own constitution is void. In yet other words, the Constitution of the United States provides that the State, in providing for the manner of appointment of electors, shall proceed according to the provisions of its own constitution. Therefore, if it can be shown that the manner provided by the legislature for the appointment of electors by a State is in contravention of its own constitution, such appointment is void under the Constitution of the United States.

Now, let us examine the constitution of Louisiana to ascertain whether the provisions of the act of 1872—if the same are applicable to the election of electors—is in conformity to, or in contravention of, the State constitution.

The constitution of Louisiana provides, title 4, article 73, as follows:

"ART. 73. The judicial power shall be vested in a supreme court, in district courts, in parish courts, and in ustices of the peace."

And then, after defining the jurisdiction of the several courts above mentioned, article 94 provides as follows:

"ART. 94. No judicial powers, except as committing magistrates in criminal cases, shall be conferred on any officers other than those mentioned in this title, except such as may be necessary in towns and cities; and the judicial powers of such officers shall not extend further than the cognizance of cases arising under the police regulations of towns and cities in the State. In any case, when such officers shall assume jurisdiction over other matters than those which may arise under police regulations or under their jurisdiction as committing magistrates, they shall be liable to an action of damages in favor of the party injured or his heirs, and a verdict in favor of the party injured shall, *ipso facto*, operate a vacation of the office of said officer."

Thus it will be seen that the constitution, not only by affirmative provisions vests the whole judicial power of the State in certain designated tribunals or magistrates, but, by negative provisions, forbids the exercise of any judicial power by others.

The sections quoted from the act of 1872 undoubtedly pretend to vest judicial powers in the Returning Board.

The highest penalty that can be inflicted upon an American citizen for crime is disfranchisement. The elective franchise is not merely a right to deposit a ballot in a ballot-box, but it is a right to have such ballot counted, estimated, and made effectual in determining the result of an election.

The 15th amendment of the Constitution provides that "the right of citizens of the United States *to vote* shall not be denied or abridged by the United States or by any State on account of race, color, or previous condition of servitude."

What would be said of the law of a Southern State which should provide that the vote of a colored citizen should be received and deposited in the ballot-box, but that it should not be canvassed or returned? Manifestly such a provision would be in contravention of this amendment. Hence it follows, that a provision of law which authorizes a canvassing board to exclude from its return any votes legally cast, is a disfranchisement of the voters casting such votes. This infliction can only be visited upon the voters by an exercise of judicial power. Consequently, any statute which authorizes the Returning Board to exclude such votes—authorizes such board to exercise judicial power—and is void under the quoted provisions of this State constitution.

Again, it is contrary to the first principles of natural justice that one man should be punished for crimes committed by another. By the provisions above quoted from this act it is provided in effect that the votes cast by a thousand honest men in a certain parish may be excluded from the canvass in consequence of violence, intimidation, or bribery committed by a thousand other men. A law which should provide that any voter who had been guilty of violence, intimidation, or bribery in an election should, on conviction thereof, be forever disfranchised, would be constitutional. But before such disfranchisement can be visited upon any voter he must be tried and convicted according to the forms of law in a tribunal possessing

judicial power to try for the crime and declare the punish-
ment. But by this act the full and extreme effect of
judicial condemnation—that is, disfranchisement—may in
effect be inflicted by a Returning Board, before whom the
voter is not summoned to appear, has no hearing, but is
condemned without appearance or hearing. A law which
provides for such consequences in such case is not only in
opposition to the constitution of Louisiana—anti-repub-
lican, opposed to natural justice—but it is too outrageous
and abominable to be tolerated in any civilized country.

2. But even conceding the constitutionality of the sections above quoted from the act of 1872, they do not pretend to confer this extraordinary power upon the Returning
Board except when a case is made under the 26th section
of the act; that is, when, accompanying the return from
the precinct, there is a statement made showing *the facts*
relating to an alleged " riot, tumult, acts of violence, intimidation and disturbance, bribery or corrupt influences, and
the *effect* produced thereby in preventing a fair, free, and
peaceable and full election, and *of the number* of qualified
electors deterred thereby; said statement to be corroborated
by three qualified electors of the parish."
It is well settled that whenever a *judicial court* exercises
a special and statutory power, outside of and apart from its
general jurisdiction, it must appear, in order to sustain its
jurisdiction, that it was acting in a case clearly within the
statute and that it strictly pursued its statutory authority.
In *Thatcher* v. *Powell*, 6 *Wheaton*, 119, the court, by
Marshall, C. J., say :
" In summary proceedings, when a *court* exercises an extraordinary power under a special statute prescribing its
course, we think that course ought to be *exactly* observed,
and those facts especially which give jurisdiction ought to
appear in order to show that its proceedings are *quoram
judice*. Without this act of assembly the order for sale
would have been totally void. This act gives the power
only on a report to be made by the sheriff. This report

gives the court jurisdiction, and without it the court is as powerless as if the act had never passed."

It is too well settled to require citation of authorities in its support ; that when a judicial court is proceeding under statutory provisions, apart from the common law, or when a special tribunal or magistrate is exercising a special statutory jurisdiction, it must appear that the case was strictly within the statutory provision, and that the course pursued was exactly in conformity with the statute conferring the authority—

" Justices' courts, not proceeding according to the course of common law are confined strictly to the authority given them—they can take nothing by implication, but must show the power *expressly given them in every instance.*"

3 *Burr*, 1366.
3 *Term Rep.*, 444.
Str., 1256.
2 *Ld. Raym.*, 1144.
Salk, 406.
Jones v. *Reed*, 1 *Johns. Cas.*, 20.
Wells v. *Newkirk*, 1 *Johns. Cas.*, 228.
Powers v. *People*, 4 *Johns. Cas.*, 292.
Blooom v. *Burdick*, 1 *Hill*, 330.
Adkins v. *Brewer*, 3 *Cowen*, 206.

In *Walker* v. *Turner*, 9 *Wheaton*, 541, it was held that when a magistrate was pursuing special authority it was " essential to the validity of his judgment and of the proceedings under it that the record should show that he acted upon a case which the law submitted to his jurisdiction."

Now, it is submitted that not in a single case in which the Returning Board excluded the vote of a parish was the foundation laid for such exercise of its authority.

To show this, let us refer to the machinery of elections in that state.

The method of holding the elections and making returns, according to law, is as follows :

The polling-place is presided over by three commissioners of election, appointed by the supervisor of registration for the parish, who is appointed by the Governor. After the balloting is concluded, the commissioners count the ballots, make two statements of the result, and deliver one statement, together with the ballot-box containing all the ballots, to the clerk of the district court of the parish, and the other statement to the supervisor of registration, together with the tally-sheets, list of voters, &c. The supervisor for the parish is required, *within twenty-four hours* after the receipt of all the statements and papers from the different polling-places, to consolidate such returns or statements, to be certified as correct by the clerk of the district court, and forward the same, with the originals received by him, to the State Returning Board; such statement and papers "to be inclosed in an envelope of strong paper or cloth, securely sealed, and forwarded by mail."

Section 43 makes it the duty of the supervisor to forward with his statement "a copy of any statement as to violence or disturbance, bribery or corruption, or other offenses specified in section 26 of this act, if any there be, together with all memoranda and tally-lists used in making the count and statement of the votes."

Section 26 provides that the supervisors' copy of such statement "shall be so annexed to his returns of elections by paste, wax, or some adhesive substance, that the same can be kept together, and the other copy the supervisor of registration shall deliver to the clerk of the court of his parish for the use of the District Attorney."

Section 26 also provides what the statement in relation to riots, intimidations, &c., shall be; that it shall be made in duplicate and under oath; and that it shall be—

(1) "A clear and full statement of *all the facts* relating thereto:

(2) "And *of the effect* produced by such riot, tumult, acts of violence, intimidation, and disturbance, bribery or corrupt influences in preventing a fair, free, peaceable, and full registration or election;

5

(3) "And of the number of qualified electors deterred by such riots, tumult, &c., from registering or voting;

(4) "Which statement shall also be corroborated under oath by three respectable citizens, qualified electors of the parish." And this section 26 also provides that the supervisor shall forward this statement with his return.

The only authority pretended to be conferred by the act of 1872 upon the Returning Board to exclude any return or statement of votes which comes within their power to canvass is in section 3 of the act, and is as follows:

"Whenever, from any poll or voting place, there shall be received the statement of any supervisor of registration or commissioner of election, in form as required by section 26 of this act, on affidavit of three or more citizens, of any riot, tumult, acts of violence, intimidation, armed disturbance, bribery, or corrupt influences, which prevented, or tended to prevent, a fair, free, and peaceable vote of all qualified electors entitled to vote at such poll or voting place, such returning officers shall not canvass, count, or compile the statements of votes from such poll or voting place until the statements from all other polls or voting places shall have been canvassed and compiled. The returning officers shall then proceed to investigate the statements of riot, tumult, acts of violence, intimidation, armed disturbance, bribery, or corrupt influences at any such poll or voting place; and if from the evidence of such statement they shall be convinced that such riot, tumult, acts of violence, intimidation, armed disturbance, bribery, or corrupt influences did not materially interfere with the purity and freedom of the election at such poll or voting place, or did not prevent a sufficient number of qualified voters thereat from registering or voting to materially change the results of the election, then, and not otherwise, said returning officers shall canvass and compile the vote of such poll or voting place with those previously canvassed and compiled; but if said returning officers shall not be fully satisfied thereof, it shall be their duty to examine further testimony in regard thereto, and to this end they shall have power to send for persons and papers. If, after such examination, the said returning officers shall be convinced that such riot, tumult, acts of violence, intimidation, armed disturbance, bribery, or corrupt influences did materially interfere with the purity and freedom of the election at such poll or voting place, or did prevent a sufficient number of the qualified electors thereat from registering and voting to materially change the result of the election, then the said returning officers shall not canvass or compile the statement of the votes of such poll or voting place, but shall exclude it from their returns: *Provided*, That any person interested in said election by reason of being a candidate for office shall be allowed a hearing before said returning officers upon making application within the time allowed for the forwarding of the returns of said election."

Thus it will be seen that the jurisdiction of the returning board to pass upon this subject at all is made to depend upon the jurisdictional fact that the return which the board receives from the parish supervisor is not only accompanied with but attached to the statement provided for in the 26th section of the act in regard to riots, intimidation, &c. If such return is not accompanied by such statement, supported by the affidavit of three electors, in regard to riots, &c., the returning board is not authorized even by this act to examine at all into the subject, much less exclude any votes. And the principle of law universally recognized that a special tribunal, as distinguished from a judicial court of general jurisdiction, can only act upon a case clearly within its jurisdiction, and must strictly pursue the methods directed by the statute in exercising such statutory jurisdiction, applies in its full force to the returning board acting under this act of 1872.

If we are right in this position, it is conclusive against the validity of the action of the Returning Board in excluding over 6,000 votes given for the Tilden electors; because the foundation for the exercise of this power by the Returning Board was not established in regard to a single parish, the votes of which were excluded by the board.

VI.

When the electoral college in this State met to vote for President, it was ascertained that two of the Hayes electors, A. B. Levisee and O. H. Brewster, had been holding offices of trust and profit under the United States on the 7th of November last, when the election for electors was held. The college considered the election as to them void ; and that, for that reason, there were two vacancies in the board. They therefore induced Levisee and Brewster to pretend to be absent, thereby believing that their absence would amount to a vacancy ; and they proceeded to fill such supposed vacancies by electing the said Levisee and Brewster to fill their own vacancies. This was a palpable sham and fraud.

But let us consider the case further. We submit that inasmuch as Levisee and Brewster were officers under the Government of the United States on the day of the election, November 7, the votes cast for them were void and as to them there was no election. In other words, the State appointed only six and not eight electors. That in regard to Levisee and Brewster, it was a case of failure to elect or appoint. Two cases are provided for by the act of Congress, (Rev. Stat., p. 21 :)

" SEC. 133. Each State may, *by law*, provide for the filling of any vacancies which may occur in its college of electors when such college meets to give its electoral vote.

" SEC. 134. Whenever any State has held an election for the purpose of choosing electors, *and has failed to make a choice* on the day prescribed by law, the electors may be appointed on a subsequent day, in such a manner as the Legislature of such State may direct."

Two cases are here provided for: one, the case of a vacancy occurring after the election ; the other, a failure to make an election. Waiving at present the question whether as between two candidates, the one receiving the greater number of votes being ineligible, his opponent is elected, in virtue of a smaller number of legal votes, and assuming that he is not, then it is unquestionable that the election is void.

In the case of the contested seat in the Senate between Vauce *v.* Abbott from North Carolina, there was a very full discussion upon this subject. Vance, who received the largest number of votes, was ineligible under the fourteenth amendment to the Constitution, and Abbott, who received the next highest number of votes and *was* eligible, claimed the seat. The Senate decided that Abbott was not entitled to the seat, and, of course, that the State had failed to make an election of Senator.

The Constitution of the United States, article 2, section 1, authorizes each State to appoint an elector, but provides that no person holding an office of trust or profit under the United States shall be appointed.

This provision of the Constitution applied to the case in hand is this : The State of Louisiana may appoint eight electors; but A. B. Levisee and O. H. Brewster shall not be appointed. Hence any attempt to appoint Levisee and Brewster is unconstitutional and void. And hence it follows that the State appointed but six electors; in other words, they failed to elect the full number to which the State was entitled. This is the case provided for by the last section quoted from the Revised Statutes of Congress, which declares that the State my by law provide for subsequent appointment. If the act of 1868 was not in force, the only provision in relation to filling such a *vacancy* was by a subsequent popular election. (Election law of 1872, section 24.) If the act of 1868 was in force, it *only* provided for *filling a vacancy* occurring after the officer had been elected. So that, whether the act of 1868 was or was not in force, there was no law of the State which authorized the appointment in place of Levisee and Brewster, as to whom there had been a failure to elect.

And therefore, in any event, two of the votes given by the Hayes electors must be rejected.

VII.

The certificate and papers returned from the electoral college to the President of the Senate show that William P. Kellogg, as Governor, issued a certificate to himself, that he had been duly appointed an elector of that State. It is well settled by the English cases, that the king, although he is the fountain of honor and of office, cannot himself exercise an office to which he might make an appointment. An appointment is like any other grant. And the same person cannot be grantor and grantee. Therefore an officer possessing the power of appointment cannot appoint himself, and a pretended appointment is void in such case.

7 *Bacon Abr.*, *Title " Offices and Officers," p.* 281.

State v. *Hoyt*, 2 *Oregon*, 246.

Peo. v. *Thomas*, 33 *Barb. N. Y.*, 287.

A sheriff cannot *certify* an excuse for his neglect, but must make his affidavit.

Rex v. *Bolton, Anstruther*, 79.

This rests upon the general principle of law that no officer can exercise the functions of his office for his individual benefit. And whenever a sheriff is compelled to rely upon his own return, made upon process issued in a cause between *other* parties, such return is only *prima facie* evidence.

2 *Greenleaf's Ev.*, sec. 585.

A distinction between the power of an officer to appoint himself to another office, and his power to issue a certificate which is conclusive evidence of such appointment, is too nice to be substantial. Therefore, to show that Kellogg was duly appointed elector, resort must be had to other evidence of the fact. At least resort *may* be had to other evidence to show that he was *not* duly appointed. The certificate of the Governor is the only evidence prescribed by act of Congress, and when, as in this instance, it is unavailing, inquiry may be made into the fact so certified

What is that fact? Why, that Kellogg was duly appointed an elector. By law the appointment can only be made by a popular election. Therefore, the question is, was Kellogg elected at the popular election in November last. This is the fact to be established; the fact that may be controverted.

VII.

This bring us to consider what evidence back of the certificate must be resorted to to establish this fact.

It will be said that the return of the canvassing or Returning Board is the next evidence to be considered, and is conclusive.

I have already shown that the action of this board is void in rejecting votes, unless a case was really in each instance according to section 26 of the Election Law of 1872; and that no such case was made in regard to any parish where the vote was excluded.

It would not be pretended that a decision of the Supreme Court of the United States would be of any avail unless accompanied by and attached to the complete record of the cause in which such decision was made. Without such full authenticated record it would not appear that the court had jurisdiction. It would be monstrous to hold that stronger presumption exists in favor of a statutory tribunal than could be indulged towards the Supreme Court of the United States. And it is submitted that to make the certificate of the Returning Board evidence at all, it must be shown that returns were made by the supervisors of registration, what these returns were, and, if the board rejected any such returns, that a case was made giving the board jurisdiction in that behalf.

We submit at least that it may be shown affirmatively that such Returning Board did not give effect to the votes as cast; and that no case was shown before them giving them jurisdiction to reject the votes. If we are wrong in this, then a fraud is as good as a fact; a judgment *corum non judice* is valid and conclusive against a party condemned; and our system of popular elections is a delusion and a snare. The voters of a State may cast all their votes for one man, and yet a Returning Board, without the slightest authority of law, may give their certificate to a person who did not receive a vote; and that certificate is conclusive upon 40,000,000 of free people.

MATT H. CARPENTER,
Of Counsel.

www.ingramcontent.com/pod-product-compliance
Lightning Source LLC
Chambersburg PA
CBHW021549270326
41930CB00008B/1426